TRACES

TRACES

A Collection of Poems

Abdou Jallow

Print information available on the last page.

Rev. date: 03/26/2019

To order additional copies of this book, contact:
Xlibris
1-888-795-4274
www.Xlibris.com
Orders@Xlibris.com
794388

ACKNOWLEDGEMENT

The dream of publishing this book would have never been a reality without the help of family, friends and loved ones. It is one thing to write and it is another to have people to pay attention and help you to be better in every way. I feel blessed to have great people around me and I will forever be grateful.

I thank my parents who are not just parents, but my friends. My older siblings too have given me the right surrounding since I was a child and believed in me since the day I started to write. It would not be sufficient to say thank you but I am wholeheartedly happy to have you all around me – my elder brothers, Essa, Buba, Salifu, Bocarr and my elder sisters, Mariama and Haddy.

Special thanks to my dear cousin, whom I see as one of my elder brothers, Bocarr Sey. You are the first person to mention the idea of publishing a book of poems to me. Thank you for believing in me. Without your encouragement and investment of your resources, this would not have been a reality.

Editing processes can be tedious and stressful. Thank you to my friends, Musa A. Jallow and Alagie M.A Jallow for giving it your valuable time and energy to analyze my work and polish it. My cousin Ebrima Sowe, one of my very best friends, thank you for putting your expertise into effort for the book cover image.

I thank my dear brotherly friend, Musa Faye. Thank you for being my number one fan, for believing in me more than I even think of myself.

I thank everyone who has been with me throughout this publishing process. My sincerest gratitude to everyone who has supported me, from newspaper editors for featuring my poems, to the people who take their precious time to read, share and review what I write. Without you all, I am useless. It would be impossible to make mention of all the people who I owe gratitude to but God knows I appreciate you all. I pray that God bless you all.

ACKNOWLEDGMENT

DEDICATION

My dear mother, Amie Sey, thank you for the unconditional love and support. There is no way that I can pay you but this is just a token to tell you that I appreciate you. I wonder what I will do without you. With all my heart, I dedicate this to you, Thank you!

CONTENTS

INTRODUCTION

"Traces" as in its literal meaning, this collection of poems is a lead to the life of mine in its entirety. Each poem herein, comes exactly as how I was feeling and thinking at that point in time it was written. It's a collection about love, sadness, happiness, just the chronicles of a person growing up. Most people keep their journals as essays, mine come in poems and here I present them as TRACES.

The oldest of the poems were written in my teenage years and the latest, at my current age. So this is like a journal of me growing up. A witness to a boy growing up to be the man. This feels like me sharing my diary with the world: stories of an African child growing up with a humble background in this 21st century.

Some of the poems aren't directly about me but, me trying to speak for a people who are forgotten. About homelessness or war for instance, are experiences I have never gone through but feel for the people going through them and speak for them.

It wasn't a plan, all the poems in here are inspired by the freewill of time. Every piece was written with the absolute inspiration from my muse.My writing style absolutely has no idea of what it is, as I don't follow any rules but pen my thoughts as they pour out in their rawest form.

Every poem resonates to a specific thing about my true being, all of them coming together tells you my full story. I hope I will inspire with my poetic story, a journey of highs and lows. Stories of mistakes and perfection I share with you. Here is to you my views about life: religion, culture, politics and social issues generally.

WALK AROUND

Greet the blossom as freshly first ever
As it witnesses day break, the wind whistling early
Walk pass, not under
Don't get cracked, too comfortable or stable
These all have got a personal motive
That you are never a part of
Once in a while, you are a plan
A planned death
Don't fall for it
Keep walking, watching and wishing
Let the truth speak
The reality will be stone-age old
Someday you will be its master
The sky was once the earth
It has no wings to fly up
So how is it watching over us?
Well, it is a fulfillment that he engulfs us

Sitting around kills
And we are too fragile
To be incarcerated in the motions of winds
Get not too pale or silent
You are a present for your life
This life of a martyr's is one to live for
Don't just be a journey but a channel to yours
Open up, walk around and die to live forever
Walk into infinity
Never stop even if you have to
Because you never need to
Walk around for you and your love

LIT THROUGH TIME

I wept in love
My heart shrinks in tears
Of joy, sorrow and I don't know what
I am through my eyes
My sight is off my side
My ego is crashed
I don't know the question
I don't know the answer Am I lost?

I am sure of being drowned
It doesn't frown me
That is my history
My longing brought me here
I thought I came a long way
Long after the age that brought him in the empire
In his tongue of Farsi
That engulfed all languages
Plainly down in the thoughts
Down with the lovers
My chest is the breast of men
Which is "fragranced" and blossomed
The golden tomb
The epitome of meaning

THE DEAD ARE LIVING

There is a sole way to live
It's through love
Love is for the living and the lovers
And those gone on the exodus
Too far, beyond right and wrong
To where who we are
Is beyond race, class and tribe
It's beauty that revolves around the universe
Safeguarding the stars that sparkle forever
Shinier as they age, watching over earth
Guaranteeing twilight
A full moon's smile
Let's go star gazing
We'll be the living of the dead

COME

Come!
Come and be, to let me be
Utter my addiction
The sound of strings
My heart when pulled
The joy of cardiac arrest
Of acoustics that ring true

When I dream and see you
I wish not to return back to this world
What is a world?
Without mindlessness
Totally wined by a heart
Deep down through time
Without feeling
Life is a painful joy

Come!
Come!
Where are you?
My mystical aroma
The sweet vibe of darkness
That makes me appreciate light
I am vulnerable and prone to catching fire
Come and light me up
We will bond forever
Burn forever
And brighten a younger age

BAYE

Whilst I walked I wondered
Asking a million questions to self
Trying to note where the ripples came forth
But then I was told to stop thinking
That it was big
But even then questions lingered
About whom I am
Where I am from
Where I am
Who brought me about?
Where is He, God?
I was asked to stop
But I couldn't
Life lived; I kept wondering
Until a voice spoke to me
It said:
None shall turn their backs on me
Except for those I do not choose

I turned and faced light
His is that voice
Took me out of wonder
And asked me to think about God
Because God never hurts
He is never too much
Nor does he stop giving answers

He, the voice, is the man
The shield of shields
He spoke all languages
As he had to do with hearts: my savior
Taught me how to swim in the big ocean
He held my hand towards the direction
And calls me to be Him
I pray to remain within this being

DOORSTEP

At your door
I will be on your steps
Open up, shake my hand
Don't just shake it, feel me
Count my pulses
Forget about me and hug my spirit
For I am a mirror when you look close
I am also a walking casket
Within a world of thin lines that hinder
Do fade those lines away
The cross lines and the deadlines
You owe them a rub
Do not be gentle

Be on your feet
And meet me at your door
Banish us together
Let us disintegrate from our solid form
That form of mine that hits on you
Is entirely just a perception
It's worldly, so I burn
Burn to light us a path beyond the curtains
So let's catch fire
Burn to ashes with all our affairs

IN A BIT

I am a bit of a mixture of wine and honey
Be mindful of your sips
Take all of me or let me be
Little of me is danger
It is misleading
It is the poison in the honey
The wine that rots you
Too much of me extract the sweetness from pain
It is the freshness in the wine
The clearing thought of that thin line
That interlinks and separates you, I, good and evil,
With and from the consciousness of existence

I don't look for your care
I am no one's business But a soul goblet
Handle me any how
Careful and reckless are all the same
Just grab and gulp me in
Get drunk of me

LATER IN THE NIGHT

It only takes being awake to see stars at night
And brighter means darker
Some unravel at such sparkle
But it breeds sleep in some heads too
Those ones who think they know
But are way wilder in their dreams
I wonder not why they talk and call us deviants
No wonder they are just stumbling in darkness

Living is beyond theory
The secret is love: the driving force
Like that ever growing desire
It leads the way forward to night time
And as we witness twilight
Black does not mean evil
If it was, nights would be sacred not
But then God is beyond color
And so his people are accepting of the rainbow
This makes the bond strong
A total fusion
In this time, is later in the night

STAR DUST

Traces of a cradle
Channels of a spirit
He said they are the doors to the city
And he is the city
Filled with light at day and night
I closed my eyes and called on to him
He left me a note
It reads:

Kiss the dust they left
I am on prints of their foot heels

It is deep!
An epitome of a being
A story of the household
That clarifies this flood
Indeed, it is real!
I dipped into reality and followed the trace
I came to the meeting point
And blessed be my dreams; about him is the truth
He came to me through death's cousin
And showed me I could be the star, through dust
How much I wish the visions came to me sooner

AFRICA

This being black
I cannot do without it's my dream
My soul, mind and spirit My mama, bless you
Africa I celebrate your being
And live your love
I love you even without your gold
I regret your woes, it's my lesson
What they have put you through
The boundaries they chained you with, irks me
But none can give you a hold
Because you are the gem

My dear mother of cradles
I see why you are so humble
For your existence is a manifestation
You are the sacred shrine of creation
You stand where none stands
Golden black, sunshine and breezes
Please rain dearest
Those drizzles shall give us life
I am only you
I can be none but you
I see them all when they fight
But your son told them 'who
Jah bless, no man can curse'

In your name, I pray that your sons know
That you are the bond, stronger and greater
Than religion, race and boundaries
Diversity is your power

And unity is your song
Culture is your heartbeat
And that is our true soul
That begets the artist
Which all your children are
Each child of yours is special
Way ahead of time
Meaning of the metaphors
The dawn and dusk of the world
My dear Africa, my spirit

OLD SONG

It hails from great rocks
Solid foundations of Sudan
It knows the great kingdoms
Or a dream of those places
This old song still plays
Mystical powers beyond modernity
Now vibrating with
This song is old but still a prayer
Epitome of something with meaning
Sense and simplicity as it came from God
With all the sparkle; it spent all its time aging
Like wine, passing time turned it better
This old song, only the third ear hears
The prayer its power ignites, only the third eye sees
And until then, when the third one grows
And you unveil the reality of your being
Keep digging and you will find the meaning
This old song says all there is

AS IN THE WORD

Out of the utterance 'be'
I was founded from dust
There I lay, hailing up
And so, I sneezed
The hiccups of my kind
The thin line
Yet an issue
The dimness of hearts
But only light makes it through
As truth lives in only one word
That brought up existence
As in the manifest,
We are only one in the same one
All there is in the utterance
And so it is
So as it will be
Like it channeled and dropped
This mighty ocean is as sweet as it is holly
The core of the word
I lay by my heart and listen
The utterance is still on
Loud and clear

WAIT

I came here open
My innocence was shoved into a cage
But wait, that's not the only hurting
Too many times I was called a coon
My eyes brimmed with tears
I wept in my heart and ran back home
But my own kind is running away from me
Conked and skinned with bleach

All the pain is not just cancer, it is self-hate
Undermining this melanin
Not a reflection on the good days buried
When we used to be what we were meant to be
A people of culture, knowledge, spirituality and wealth
It's darkening our future
This is not the Nubians way
This is self-made inferiority

But wait, are you hearing me?
And you still wish not to do anything about it
It's your time and your being
And only you can do something about it
Because only you care about yourself
All else just care about your wreckage
Your pain is their only gain
I am sure you are just too naïve
But not too dumb to give up on yourself so low
Live black
Your melanin is your truth

TARRED PEARLS

I am into my memories
Like a wagging tail but not of the lion's
This is more of me shaking my head
I agree with my flaws
And admit all that I have been
My preciousness is drawn from a pool of tar
At boiling point, I make this hard road
As black as it is far and bumpy

And when I do take this road
Derailing is not a choice
Because there was never another option
There is one way to go and it cares about no sin
In fact, a sin and blessing are like two different
solutes in the same solvent

No distinguishing between the water and the poison
You cannot call it 'without a cause'
As it is all done for the sake of survival but is it worth it?
If life is more than gold
Then why not just live where living is free
But again freedom is questioned!
Where has it gone?
Why do circumstances decide who one becomes?
These questions are rhetoric

Still bringing more questions than answers
This whole world is in jeopardy
I am thorn in this journey
Caught in this snare of 'trying to make it'
Death is not an option

As I am not too ready to face my sins
So I hope the Lord will pardon me
Until I make it, I am in the making
Cleansing and bringing back the
preciousness of my once a being
Being of pearls, so clean as it used to be pure

I AM HERE

I am here, ripped of my blood
I give up every attribute
I am alone with my heart
A conversation where the mind has no place
For it can only think
But the heart and soul know how to feel
Every beauty, sense and subconscious reality is here
No boundaries to the flows
And thus, life means only living

Who else has verses in mind?
Like that glass full of pristine
I need a drink that shall have me freed
Purely divine and takes me high: highly drunk
And unconscious of this world
This rusty crust that just give me tetanus
Who knows where we can be?
That place within us
The stand-alone flower in my garden

I have my gates open to this field
I have chosen to welcome you
I just hope that you will come in bare
And breathe me al fresco
Feel it
Do not intoxicate it
Where someone is better than words
Sweet words, romantic and all you call it
Are one way of hatred
The way they can drive a heart far

Can be contrary to the reality
It's a swing over the sea of suicide
How best can you save such
Other than with your silence?

Silence is better than misleading speech
It gives thou time to face your sins
Who is ready to hang a picture?
Of us showing the world our back
Without a plan but just a desire
Caring not about perfection of whatsoever people think
But dipping in our sincerity
And writing our story
Caring not if it rhymes
But that it reflects the truest of times
Like am telling you
Answer me only if you speak your heart

THIS IS WHAT YOU ARE

The shell that embodies the core of purity
An outcome of an "Amen"
The vision in the eye
The direction of prayer
The symbol of freshness

Oh! you are the secret between dawn and dusk
You are the bond, the cover
The big heart of life
The confidence of secrets
I whisper your name
And it means resistance
Persistence
Perseverance
Content
And love

You are energy and a force greater than the shackles
The interruption of your history
That you have risen from
You never choose to despair
And thus it was never too late
Even though it was too hard
You stood up
And up and strong as you are,
You shall forever be
As you are the seeing in the eye
So your vision makes this world go around

FOR THAT BEING

She is the love that hovers
As the blanket over my head
And let me be a secret here and there
Later and time older
She, the beauty of darkness
That lets me dream when I can see not
And preach peace
Which invokes incense
To sweeten my soul
As life is lived

She plays, smiles and sheds tears
Tears made of honey
From the depths of her heart and all what
there is,
It is persisting
Till the beauty swallows the full moon
That of her darkness
Of coffee, chocolate and night
Which gives birth to twilight
My dwelling rejoices as I am her sun
Totally fused
In this being of Layla

REVISITING THE GREAT CIRCLE

I revisit a memoir: the book
I miss brethren, uncle, aunty and sister
When I think of granny, I become a loner
I cry, but then I am comforted reminiscing
About the jokes she told

Teaming with dear brother
And cherished cousin, we built an empire
It was a time that watched our dreams from scratch
Time and space brought us far
Now, all is missing in the puzzle
But no page tears from the book
The book which is a heart
The single heart we have in common
Defeats the distance
Through a bridge of feelings
Strong connections, stronger than us
The unconditional love within and around
If found, once more

Time still inspires hope
A dream that sees a belief alive
That someday, somehow
History will repeat
Memoirs will resurface
We'll all meet at grandma's dome
Someday, we will eat lunch together
Under the mango tree and drink green tea
Be a bigger and better a family

TEA OR COFFEE

Your bitterness is the sweetness of my aroma
Your blackness is what makes the sacred a secret
Of course, the secret is scared
You are summary of time
Your strength is simplicity
You only fit in the head of the humble
For you are an outburst
That reminds me of the tiniest atom
Simple yet reflecting creation
The cell of holiness
As it is in the depths of seas
The surface of shores
The outlines of horizons
And the height of mountains

You are a blessing to the human race
Company of the scholastic
Through which ancients can be traced
You know the sunrise of tomorrow
As you witnessed many of a Layla
Sainthood is aware of your taste

Your humility, the shallow minds mix up
They call you an addiction
I know you are beyond addiction
Because you are love
The affair in every culture
The connection of different classes
You are the muse
As sweet as you are black
I honor you for your being of me
With me, for me
All the way

DEAR SON

Sun, when you shall rise tomorrow
Shine as you watch over the Nile
As you shine, be mild
Not too extreme
Remember it's a day of mine
The seed of my yesterday
You, my sun, are the hope
The little precious plant
Bearer of the flower
That you are the bright light
That charges up the moon
After dusk, for a brightly smiling Layla
It shall be a guarantee
For dreams to be born
Dreams to feed the dreamers
The twinkling star
The charming beauty of twilight
The tears of love only I wish them to shed
Shed the heavenly light on their foreheads
Reflection of might
Fulfillment of prevalence
Hearts filled with the highly sought
Until then, keep calm
Be the being of the sun

LIT THROUGH TIME

I wept in love
My heart shrank in tears
Tears of joy, sorrow and I don't know what
I am over my over eyes
My sight is off this side
My ego crashed
I don't know the question
Neither do I know the answer
Am I lost?
I am sure of being drowned
It doesn't make me frown, though
That is my history

My longing brought me here
I thought I came a long way
A long way after the age
That brought him in the empire
In his tongue of Farsi
Which engulfed all languages
So plain in thoughts
Down with the lovers
My chest is the breast of men
Which is fragranced and blossomed
The golden tomb in my heart's garden
The epitome of meaning

SATIRE

In your eyes, the deviant is on the right path
You could have listened to a word
Before you did spread words
Words about one word
And that's the truth
You say the truth is deviation
How about listening him?
If you really believe in him
He knows more about himself
Much more than how you feel in your own heart

The wrong is the yardstick
A pool of emotions
That's just a mirror between you and the truth
And it appears showing your being
Which is not what you ought to seek
Ponder on the image, ask about the truth
He will tell you about breaking the mirror
that's when you will then see beyond
You will find and drink the sacred from the goblet

Until then, don't stop
Refresh!
Have good faith in each one
Because greatness doesn't speak
It's a vibe and it's only drawn by humility
The low images in your eyes
They are not thugs as you judge
They have seen light
And not the words you spread
The truth knows them
He dwells in them and has the same nerves

BETWEEN LIFE AND DEATH

Between life and death, there is love
Between love and hatred, there is life
Love kills weakness, breeds bravery
Comes up with defense
To stand up for a belief
The strong faith against wrongdoing
Fatally costly
But I rise up to the bully

Kill me once
You can't do it twice
You can silence me
But never take the man out of me
You can take my today
But tomorrow I will die for
The difference in men is dignity
I owe it to generations
So I'll pay infinitely
Take these serious times seriously

This life is the love of my life
I'll go beyond miles
To be surrounded with smiles
Living dreams
And flourishing days
For my being a son, is my truest
A flower for those gone
Respect to the holding on
For freedom, we shall reign

WHAT MATTERS

I am just one of a dream
A song and a tear
An inspiration, a rose
I don't know if I am a red or white rose
But just lay on a casket
Of the fallen soldier to heaven
Rest my ear to what is said
I am a conveyance of what's to be
What I feel is right
And it doesn't matter if it's a rebellion
The matter is what matters
And it is what makes us different
In races, classes and nationalities
The long standing gold coated walls
But yet with a rusty core
I stand to break them
I don't know if they are too strong to break me
But I'm sure I want to be the bridge
That would kill the distance
And bring limbo into light
Whatever it means, is my struggle

FROM ME, FOR ME

Rhymes are punching through
In and out of my cranium
It's about pain and joy It's sweet pain
And makes me feel light from the outside
Feeling weightless and nothing important

Inside and outside
Breaking me but irresistible joy
Bundling up my pieces
Tie them more to it, I will be the sweat
The scarce liquid in the rocks
To water 'the rose that grew from a concrete'

When I am hungry, sad and shattered
Only words can feed me
Comfort me and build me up again
Without ego
Letting go and learning
Lean not on luck but work
Until when pain turns to ease,
Only words can bring me peace

NEW AGE

Every day lies in a struggle
Every need to buckle is to pass the huddle
Because life has turned to what it wasn't meant for

Life was supposed to be presence
A creation which reflects on the beauty that they are
Attract their powers
And blend with their purpose, worship nothing

But it is darkness
The age of smart gadgets
And lost people
Craving for the world
Ending up being just a thing
Lover of the outer most
Deeply wounded, internally bleeding and dying

THROUGH WORLD

I'm fed up with living
And they still ask me to keep trying
I don't care about the lessons and trials they try to teach
Neither the bright day that they promise
Because all along this world found it pleasing
To serve us facades on the plate

This living is boring, it kills my interest
And when I reverse, I go nowhere
There are no memories
That can give me the comfort that I need
Just the same hollow of a life
That can't just let me be

I chose to keep it to myself
But then I lost it again
All the advices, the prayers and the sermons make me sick
Why should I believe in destiny?
I mean their definition of destiny
Is suffering and believe in empty promises
That everything is heavenly
That there is a life coming
But how sure are we that it's ours?

Even if you are wrapped in blossoms
God knows that you are a rusty core
And even if you are soaked in rose water
He knows you are sweating
Stop pretending and talk to him

Don't just believe in the vainness
Ask him and he will give you reason
Beyond your believe in destiny
And there comes the ultimate freedom
Get free from fear

SON OF THE MOMENT

I discovered myself
Through trends
Of sweetness and pepper rubbed in a fresh wound
And honey finding my taste buds
Pleasing and hurting
Going and coming
Loud and silencing

I am made of days
I am unknown
Frozen and broken
Melted, molded and forged
A black gold
And sweet honey

I make joy and grief
But turn sadness to happiness
See heaven even in the midst of hell
I am part of the living
And live the whole through me
As I am through it
I am son of the moment

ME

I am made of honor that I can never sell out
Betrayal is my horror
Secrets, I would never
shout
I walk through this corridor
Guided, so I would never miss out
My being is that of a lover's
My blackness makes me proud
Not racist
My religion makes me humble
Not intolerant
In fact, what is the sense in race and religion
If it doesn't make us feel any good?
It is all here to make our blend beautiful
Like the rainbow, different colors mean beauty
So, I rejoice this in me
Forever bow to the master
And say his name aloud
Loud in both my heart and by my tongue

TO CUPID

Dear Cupid
I am not stupid
To tell you the truth,
There is only one way
And it's beyond you
I am too rocky for your arrow
You cannot bring me sorrow
I am your master
You can never lead me
Like all those hearts you stab in the back
I shall end your reign
I am the king

Love is true
But when it is twisted, it becomes an obsession
And thus misleading
This will awfully deviate its purpose
Because love is divine
And should be a mutual thing
Instead of bringing suffering
And making your beloved an idol
Love should be the "thanks" you give
And the joy which make you give thanks
To show gratitude to the one that brought you love
And nothing else of worshiping your love
It will be like worshiping your wishes
How can you imagine that?

THE HARD WAY

I didn't know it
I was carried away
Brought into this way
I'm just another victim
I had to learn the hard way
On this back way
With the best teacher – experience
Sad that my life is the practical
Of what knows not a future
A heart's fracture that would never heal
Everyday makes it sourer
With the truth of immigration laws
Visa is a violation of human rights
That deepen its claws in freedom
Are we all not citizens of this world?
If animals can travel without borders
Then why can't we
Where we are the masters of creation?

WHEN YOU SEE CLOUDS

At some point,
You could only see clouds
You expected rain
To come with cool air
Wash away your fears
And make you realize your dreams

You knew not what clouds are made of
Is it water?
But it could be smoke
Or yet just dust
With a powerful tornado

You just saw clouds
You anticipated rain
To blossom your garden
But rain can come with thunder
Lightening and heavy winds
This can crush you to death

So when you see clouds again
They may be smoke
Dust so powerful
In as much you brace up
For the rain that you wish for,
But be ready for other cases too

DESERT MYSTIC

A voice and a heart
The only surviving
Breathing out in the dry winds
The life in the oasis
The shade in the desert
Freshness in spirit
The people who were not in flesh
But indeed have heard the message
And seen through this light
Of the sun that has risen from the west

GHETTO PROPHET

From the gutters to the slums
Under the bridge and on the beach
From Nairobi to Serbia
As far as Sao Paolo and India
A people of generations
Buried on sidelines
Off the sights of considerations
Responsible for this life that they never made

Coke, Rum and pot
Intoxicated minds
Dying hearts with dreams
The brother is a daddy
And the sister a baby mama
Circumstances make them who they are
But they still thrive through hell
Getting up from the dirt
And still choose to dream
Even where tomorrow will never beam

Every day is a test
Everyone is a hero for being today's witness
Ends never meet
And in lieu of solving their problem,
They are jailed, shot and murdered
For resorting to the only way out
Rapping, sniffing and puffing
To escape from this time

YOU AND I

I am a Muslim; a Sufi
You have problem with it?
My life is your solution
I will deal with you, with who you are
I shall judge you not
But understand that we are beings
And the overwhelming power that I feel
Makes me dumb to what they castigate you for
And tells me more of truth
Of who I am
That I should hold on to this

This "blazing star" is burning indeed
May it burn down the tiniest feelings and thoughts of us
Thoughts that are wrong
Don't let me calm down
But dissolve in this deep sea we are in
The sea of love;
Blindness and mindlessness in feeling
The truest of our essence
We are nothing where we can speak or do
But a master when we realize it
I hope you will feel the coolness of this sea
That only there is
And throw your whole being of nothingness
Embrace existence
Catch fire and burn to ashes

IF I WERE YOU

I would break all the glasses to see
What life truly is
The core of the truth is deviation
Because what is trending, what is assumed to be right
Is just distraction

If I were you
I would stop asking
Know that the answer is me
That I am the problem
That I am the solution

If I were you
I would know that I am the master
Master of my time
That I am what I make
There is no present, past and future
But only my being

If I were you
I would stop living this life
Of fearing death
I will make tomorrow today
I will see no more success or failure
So I will live without fear to fail
But mind only my sincerity

A THOUSAND LAUGHS

Listen to the creeping sound
Tickling, but somehow deadly
As it turns the hearing deaf
And closer to meaning without explanation
For its simplicity like the basics
You wouldn't just understand
For your intelligence thinks it's superior to think

A thousand yards, like deep in the woods
Counting shrubs and lost in time
Burning the mats, kissing life
Feeling the joy
As the truth slowly come
It matters not how slow
But it's the truth
And so be it

Smiles of one man in reflections
Of three but one being
Of three but a hundred times
The truth is in three hundred smiles
Each a tongue with a laugh
Out loud in the most of consciousness, a thousand laughs

ALL WE

All we kissed is this earth
But without roots
We sounded a gem
But all through this wind
I am the master
And here you are, mistress of my illusions

All we knew sounded so great
So much in the echoes
As we reflected only in each other
We were just trapped
Entangled in our yearnings
But something indeed is better
We are the blossom
But fail to see the flower in us
Our union is a confusion
A diffusion of mistakes
We are breathtaking
But just stylish failure

We are a witness to no testimony
Vain in meaning
That I would like to get more drunk
Feel no more this earth
Never the same through me again
And never through it
Let's stop this and do it

TO WHOM IS GOING

To the sea in deepness
Where there is no horizon
No sea and the shore
But the ocean throughout creation
Where we don't know you and I
But just being us in spirit
Where we will never split for there is no diverging power

Come on
Come
Welcome to infinity
You are the way forward
The rider and the ride
The here, there and where
Fly so you wouldn't be trapped in this world
But this universal truth that you are
You are what you are, let you live the reality

Life has only life to offer
Death is just an illusion
Deeds will never come to an end
They will follow you like a pendulum
Your pleasures are not for you
But entirely your wrath
It will hunt you when you choose to die

Come on
Come to wake
This life is like a circle
There are only boundaries
You can live only within
Deep in yourself, burn your energy
Let go of you and live
You are freedom

ALL NIGHT IN DAY

If God was having me tested
Then, I'm afraid that I'm busted
Because so much time I've wasted in this life
Like my patience and faith have turned too diminished
My fate is in thin air
No hope, or slim like a hair strand
Gasping and grounded
Finding my way in this hidden day
Where am I in this world?
There are no more blossoms
Eden is deserted
The roses are frowning
And the birds are pulling carts
The sun, only a glimpse
Like a minute old day
No time to dry my hay
I have not but a choice to stay
Stay and cry all night and day

FOR TOMORROW

I wanted to weep and throw all out
I wanted to vent
Be whatever being
Caring not about the future
But time has a story to tell and that holds me back

Time will tell
And in case I vent,
My child will be born living my life
My empty chest will fill his breast
Like a war cemetery, the end of brave men
Forever cast him as the outcast

I maintain my silence
So that in case I'm gone,
I will take all sins with my soul
So he will live like a child and grow to be a man
Tomorrow is too precious for the sun not to rise
So I shred and take it all in the name of time, me and my son

REFLECTION

In the end, we are the end
There is no time where life is not
Life is in beyond the curtains of death
It is all reflection;
The image, the body and the mirror
We are within beyond
And beyond is within us

So where do we go?
What's our view?
The way is one
There is no color
There is no sky
There is no planet
But the universe of those living

Your death be your birth
And your birth be your death
Your demise be your life
Be born in every day
Greatness is in rebirth

KNOCKING

All hopes are blinded
Which way to go is in limbo
I want to fly
But my wings are broken
These storms are retarding my walk
Night is turning to day
And dreams are being nightmares

I have it all to gamble
The core in my chest
Bursting my breast
Beating, whipping and knocking
All dead around
I am bored and lonely with life
The new is old
So nothing is a surprise
More of intensity and friction
Rubbing me with roughness

HERE YOU COME AGAIN

I am so vulnerable
Like a cheese on the table with fire approaching
Silenced and humbled
Her hunger on me she will stumble
I will not be poisonous
But not too soft if you will want me

Here you come again
I am like a wobble bubble
A hobby for granted
Last if wanted
Never access granted
But my heart experimented
Leaving my heart so intoxicated

Here you come again
I don't have a clue of reasoning
Toxics have saturated my being
It's the honey that makes me drunk
Honey is alcoholic in your case
Looking with no sight
My heart is taking me to the wrong side?
Well sadly, I look up to you to come

JE NE SUIS PAS CHARLIE HEBDO

I am not against freedom of speech
But advocate too for responsibility of speech
I am not in support of darkness
But compromise not tolerance
I am not at peace with the offence
But condemn the reactions with the killings of innocence
With no guidance from the master
I am not a stand-alone
But a Muslim and obliged to echo the truth
I am not going to terror
But reflect on divinity and hail for perfection

REIGN OF HYPOCRISY

There is injustice in justice
That shell that keeps us within words
That we are so wrong
Judging with guidance from partiality
Intentionally intensifying the killing of minds
In the name of freedom
With no definition of what's freedom
And no sense of responsibility
The world is like we don't care of the lives
But just upper hands keep pressing
As innocence is bleeding, crying
And endlessly stabbed in the back

THE MOMENT

The moment has come
The moon is polished
The stars are gathering
Twilight is here
The wind is fierce
Blowing eastwards
And the doves are wavering
Even the volcanoes and oceans of the wildest are calm

In smoothness of the wool
That calm touch between my skin and the bed
My pillow is so damp
With tears from my heart
Draining my thinking
I don't own my mind
It's the subject of my heart

These tears of love
I wish the earth in Madinah is my place
In the hands of the father

In this day
The birthday of all creation
Oh this leaves me so cold
As the burning desire gets stoked
The more I see
The more I hear
 The more I feel
Makes this yearning grow

Let me just live the moment
In this quest to get close
In the loud and sweet of voices
Follow the traces
And chant praises
For the beloved:
May peace be upon him

HUMANE

How about we avoid poor justification of mistakes?
Before we jail them,
Why not question the roots of their reasons?
It could be trauma...

Have you obliged religion?
This is guidance
That molds the living with tolerance
And resort to a free world
The true word
That we ought to live

I tell you that I see an end
To terrorism, racism, and fascism
For if we know where we are from,
The path ahead will be bright
And our differences bridged
This is a humane world

FORWARD TO DAWN

Ten voices, each has a different wish
Goodies lavished
Repenting and praying
 Forgiving and forgiven
Open hearts and mind
In one soul, all live
Buckling in belief, there shall be peace
Let the rocks turn to gold
Tic toc! Fireworks in place,
Not just a new year but a dawn to true success!

BUFFALO RIDE

By the cold
We stood in the dark
Warmed up in an atmosphere of dreams
We kept warm in that ghetto vibe
You know, 'Babylon'

We took it by the horns
But it unsettled with a storm
Well time moved on
We went with life
I still am not sure what's happening
I thought the wishes were never answered
But then it's destiny
Dreams are dying
And I wish to crumble
It's like am back in my cradle

I'm still in the same jacket, in the same jeans
Trying to avoid this unavoidable feeling: I still try
But then I'm no member of an academy
And they say I have to be schooled first
But my bag of gold is empty
Where education is a business

I still choose to go
But they say, I have to hold on to my belief
Determination is void
Because am inexperienced
I managed to live this long
Life's been an adventure

For belief,
I wish not to wear the jeans ever again
Nor the jackets
And being the jack at the junction
I don't want to be squashing the dreams
I don't want to be at a dead-end
I wish a year is on the way
I wish next December I wouldn't be asking "Wagwaan?"

BELOVED

The eastern sun
Before you rose
You were the west, north, and south
After you rose
You are still the west, north, and south
You are the soothing star
You are older than time
You are calmness
Master; you are beauty
You are consciousness
You are the heart
The flavor in sweetness
The seeing in the eye
The feeling in the senses
The living in life
The energy in ability
The brightness in light
The will in goodness
The marvel of creation
The shield
The peace in peacefulness
May I be confined in your path

YEARNING TO PRAISE

I have so much longing
This is a worry
Ages have passed
And it brought no identical century old twins
They have such countless voices
As sweet as heavenly spring
Like wine, sweetness comes with age

This has taken me afar
A state of drunkenness
So much so I beg for just a word
But it has gone with all that have been said

Might give me reason
I give all for a praise
I am starved and severely thirsty
Even though much I tasted
But it is gone with all that has been said

Like you hold everything
I behold and pray in your name
In the wilderness,
It is the old city,
To the ancestors and the unborn
All I wish is a song
I wish there will be one to express this deepness
The beloved, only you I can yearn for

WAKING UP TO LOVE

I woke up loving, I tried to see
But darkness owned the room
I tried to get up
But ability was still asleep
I wished to breathe
But the air was intense
I yearned to drink
But there was only rose water

I tried to think but it was all about love
That speaks loud
And then whispers
That is so blind
And I know it's dumb

I couldn't but follow the trend
I was conditioned
I wished to be human
And love posed as a way out
It's indeed the way out
To malfunction; extreme senseless mission
A matter of living dead
Like a feather standing as a flower

Love is pain
It makes you unconscious
And hums only to its wishes
Like dreams and fantasies
Never looking back or forward
Just walking without direction
And setting about you all on fire
Love is leading to nowhere if it is obsession
So beware!

TAKE IT EASY

See them like you
Yesterday when your thoughts were foolishly wise
Your vision blindly revolutionary
And your ears so choked,
You moved ahead
You were seen
You were given ears
 As you tried to be

Hear him as you wished to be heard
Like when you were five
You never knew who you wanted to be
But you played
Through days you found sleep
And so you dreamed

Don't say that it's nonsense
Let them play
Because that's how a child discovers himself
The boy is a man
The girl is a woman
They are the minds of tomorrow
You be the architect
Let them grow So take it easy

MY BEING

Mind and soul, I'm black
Flesh and blood, I'm African
Thoughts and feelings, I'm positive
Life and death, I'm sincere
To the young and old, respect
Faith comes first
I'm eternally a servant
I love hard
So I go hard
To what comes next,
Is a matter of living

POETESS

She ought to be like I am
I will be the best of what is meant to be

We will be the blossoms
Live in mist
We will not want to know
What says this world

The sand dunes await
Where we will rest
As we go deep
I will listen
Let you rhyme
To what will bond us
The meaning of love
That's not child's play
And I will ponder

Come on
Come and become
A mighty sea of wind awaits
Let's swim through the atmosphere
In words we will be huddled not
Come on poetess
Where are you?

HAMATTAN

Whistling winds
So straight and fierce
Greetings from the Sahara
Send my regards

You know the rain flooded
As we got soaked in blessings
Moments of prayer
Shuts my eyes and I whisper

I pray
Let me stay
That you are clement
And let through you
Run the blessings of my being
Let's go to what I hail

FRACTURED

My heart is never broken
It's fractured
Like it was never solid
Just a sponge of mud
A spank with tears

Go to the paddy
The shallow roots are my seed
Plant and I will grow and blossom
You will see me
When you look after me

Do you wish to follow me?
I will only feed you with blood
You will be a cannibal
You are so pretty to be such
So take a bite of me
Keep it deep in your thoughts
But maybe I am not even worth remembering

AB'BUL ABBAS

The esteemed creatures
To their being as they swim
Where heights are in depths
Thou is light
The core of the shield
The dawn at dusk
The sweetness in Layla

All the greatness
That enchant these creations
Is it not grudge?
That they grumble
About what is so plain

The sky knows not your height
Oceans too shallow to exist
The ancient is unaware of your youth
Like the present and tomorrow
Are too ignorant for your demise

The only vein in my heart
I wish not to serve my being
But strive to get close
To you more than the way my heart is close to me
And way beyond my mind

The hidden in you
The secret of the sacred
My trodden path
Let me be yours For your sake I live
I seek to know you
Like the way you wish
That none knows how to wish

WHERE DO WE GO?

In lieu of the craving
It should be a pondering
The way forward
From here onwards

Do you know he is crying?
The regrets over his deeds
Were just sins
Backed by trends
And he went on as yesterday

Halt
Where do we go?
Continuing the journey
That yesterday started
Is it so bright ahead?

Turnaround
From night to day
Let's go onshore and start over
An empire that will see tomorrow
Is where you end violence against her
Let's go there!

LOVER'S WISH

Dear Lord
Whenever the time comes
And shadows emerge,
Intense the heat enough
Let the sun burst
Show no twilight
Incarcerate me in the earth
Like six feet deep

I dare not to be the imbecile
That is on exile
From his own land
With the will to love
But not the beloved
He loves not
Is he who loves the seen

So Lord
Count my words
Take me out of my mind
Fill me up
Up through your door
As I shut my eyes
And wish to get drunk
Wish to get lost
Hold my hand
And lead me away
I will be at peace when I die
But only through deep love for the shield

I AM OUT OF WORDS

But I need to say this
It is burning
I am at blaze

I need to write a will
But I've got three words

In spite of everything
I shall forgo and trade these words
I will whisk them for you
And get drunk

Take them
For 'I love thee'
Engrave them on my tomb
My three words are gone
I am out of words; I am gone

TELL ME

Make me believe
I will let you convince
Now is your chance
So you confide

Tell me!
Tell me that I am alone
Where you cannot see
That strengthens not
What your love entails

That straightforwardness
Deep in your glittering pupil
Come on, I want to see
A reflection of my demise

Come on tell me
Tell me that you don't love me
Even if you do
Because it will let me be at peace

WHY DO WE CRY?

My eyes are so sour
But this is like in the ocean
That turns the eyes rosy
As red as it feels
As the heart filled with blood
But in love
You know when it turns to pain?

It is like so plain
But beyond words
Like a rupture
Of a lover's strive
Thriving in solitude
Oh! this mounts have eyes

I cry but wonder
Why do you cry?
How do you cry?
If you never loved
And that's why we cry

GOLDEN CALIBER

Tipped blunt
A black flow
Traced in lines
Shedding light
For thoughts

Secrets in the open
Shiny like the mirror
Reflecting views
Fading certainties
For what is within
Never unfolds

Erected skyscrapers
With words as the building blocks
Solid to strike
With spite and enthusiasm
Standing bold in calibers
On peaks and valleys

From hearts;
Heart touching
From minds;
Striking back solid
A replica of an image in every dome
With difference in views

LINGERING THOUGHTS OF EXISTENCE

A sudden buzz; Fuzz
Endurance of time
Never ending moments
Junks of thoughts
Reminiscing days
Mimicry of truth
Hard to bare
Drowned in despair

Questioning my stare?
Step on these stairs
It shall be your admittance of emptiness
A great deal of dust
Hiding my view
Within this crew
Mob of nothingness

In search to quench my thirst
Goblet in a quest
Fetch the droplets
Of condensed mist
Before dusk

The scriptures read aloud
My thoughts cleared
Without doubt
In motion with time
Will I end the quest?

WHILST YOU ARE GONE

Even when the clocks freeze
There would be a breeze
A feeling of what time will tell
And all how you fell, will be felt

Whilst you are gone
Our memories live on
I will shed tears not
A reflection of your blessed company
But send you verses
That you have the roses

When you are to be missed
I shall not miss thee
For my heart knows
Where you live in me
That will never die
 Even whilst am gone

Until we meet,
Where we shall meet,
May it be sweet
And again let us again do it
Until then,
RIP grandfather

GATEWAY

I am not digging
To find any of what it looks like
Comparison is not my dream
I just wish to shed light
Through this prism
So you will see the colors
Defying not to the rainbow

This realm is my reality
The flowing spring
In abundance of sweetness
That through me it runs
So I cherish
And wish to say beyond thanks
For my gratitude
Is beyond that magnitude of words

Indeed the skies know
What I mean when I call you
For they know who stood in me
That temporal greatness
A bump in the journey

I still wonder where
I still wonder what
I still wonder when
Can I find the right caliber
To write to you
In the perfect language

That none ever spoke
And manifest the depths
That I cannot even tell
What in this world means
But to live
So God bless the sunset
My gateway to my time on this path

ZEALOUS

Now I wish to be
Recognizant in the heart
As already on the face of earth
And the sun
The rain
The wind
The stars
The moon
Be heard where I am seen
On this journey

Bare me witness
As I confess
The fuel of mine
Is beyond the mind
So as the burning fields
My ego is gone

My view vanished
My feeling is no more
My sense is just frozen
I am monopolized
My vision is God
So I reignite my zeal
And carry on to the ultimate

FETCH

In his words:
It is evidently your engravings
That you need not to be needy

So I have to get immersed
And go deep
Further than this ocean's bed

The glitters are the diving suites
The connection to the manifestation
That will take me there
Are the golden beads
Oh this diamond of the ocean
Of my black heart
I give in offering

I give it away with my life
The life of needs and river blindness
With my every breath,
I give up anger, happiness and embrace death
Just to leave for good
And live forever without limitations

I AM

I am Muslim where I am poetic
I am poetic where I am Muslim

I am six feet deep where
I am seven skies high
I am black where I stand
And I stand for where I am black

I speak when I am in prayer
I am in prayer where I speak
I am in silence where I speak
And I speak in the name of my Lord

DEAREST

Love of my love
Lover of my heart
The depths of my beauty
The realm of my goodness
The cream of my heaven
My heaven, my mummy

How can I ever grow in your eyes?
When being your toddler is the greatest blessing
The amazing grace of your arms around me
Let's me know what ought to be sought
The divine rule, not the dividing rule

How can I ever grow without this presence?
The strongest where I am weak
Where I hold on when all slips off
You have all to give me hope
My strength
My reason
Giving me reason to love
Not to hate

How can I never love this being unconditionally?
My world,
My reflection
I look on to you
And pray, so God will answer
To my huge heart for you
Only you, my dear mum
God knows my love
May he bless this.

FORTUNE TELLER

If thy name really implies its meaning
What does a future hold?
For a supposed murderer
You are not to tell
If thy name truly mean fortune

Where did you get the fortune?
Of such a name that ignites optimism
But frightening to hear
Hear about both ups and downs
Of what time still hasn't beget

I only wish one wish from thy fortune
Sake my hand
And don't read my palms
Let me go with zeal
Rather than the fear to fail
Or count my eggs
And put them all in your basket
Of just promises of you alone
Don't blindfold me

LUSTY

The lusts are ill
Like a man in the midst
Of the ocean without a gill
Gasping to reap some good
But blindfolded

Mimics
Mumbling and jumbling
Heading in gallops
Oh lord they have turned blind eyed
May they see in earnest
For the Lord is all for the needy

BETTER SOMEWHERE

I knew this world had something better
So I took a walk lonely
I pictured somebody
In the old castle she is
But far in the sky
As I kept walking,
She kept going
So I started to fly

Days took me
Right in front of the castle's entrance
I knocked and knocked
To the extent of stabbing the doors
But I still stood alone
I had to pray
My only chance to pray in my life,
I prayed to her

Dawn and dusk swallowed each other
My orientation started to come alive
Where I can't say no more
Left with nothing to say
I could only do little, Breathe, wait and yearn

She came near
I stood up and gave thanks
But now in regrets
For she is not the lady
But the castle girl

Oh no! I have to go
This girl looks like the church girl
I was looking forward to a lady
And revelations say
Ladies live not in castles
Castles are just in my mind
And I will have to get rid of the thought

BOW

Oh I wish I was poetic enough
Just to scribble one line of my feelings
It would be a love burst
Splashes shiny enough
Golden brush scripts
That would let me grow
Older than time
Further than space

This joy it brings
I bend down low
And replicate what he adored
My word of praise;
Secret of secrets
Sacred of the sacred
The exclamations in the sermon

If I could utter just a word
It will be a word of praise
I choose to love
And pray to know
I wish to be born
Let me realize

IMMATURE VERDICT

They heard me say:
Do you have an idea
Of what's it like
When we head for mars on Sundays?

My words they never pondered on
Declared without my consent,
That I adhered to the trinity
When in my speech, I meant the planet
All they heard was the mass
And they chose to judge instead of asking me
Now, how could they help even if I was wrong?

If you cannot understand,
How can you judge?
In fact, why are you to judge?
Your purpose is to mind yourself instead
Because every man is his own responsibility

Dear lord,
Give ears
Give them sight
Then they will see light And tell if we are right

MURK

Sparks can only be bright
They can burn too
When they light your way
Be you
Seek sight
If you can't see, switch sight
Do what is right;
Don't take sides
I mean show tolerance

It can show a great deal of might
But not at night
Because it hasn't absorbed enough
Light to survive the darkness
Only in the rain it stands to be washed clean
And then try to build walls
Don't be fooled
For never can it protect your worlds
So mind your words

This murk is just mist
That only hinders your view
In not being tolerant
Trailing on the traces
Of what should have been the savior
But you are so cold
In your head, heart and soul
All it is the murk

ENOUGH IS ENOUGH

For long it's been a free ride
Greedily grabbing us in slices
Caring not for mutual ties
But only your part to survive
All fed with lies
So your pastures turned greener

Don't call it an escape,
We stood and freed our cape
We chose love instead of hate
All the mystery in the grave
We will not forget but forgive

We don't forget
So we will never fall in the pit
For our downfall that you dig
As a people, no more we pull in
But for our tomorrow we give in
For we have never been sleeping So, we rise!

AMEN

Just
The straight path of the praised ones
Die for
Just to live
Incarnated and dissolved
In knowing
The sacred;
The first,
The last,
The hidden,
The shown

Wisdom
Light; inner and outer glow
The virtue
The day in the days
On the height of heights
In the footprints
Which embossed on the hardest of rocks

May I realize
Relish and revolve
Within and bridge my being
Fix the dots
To the only dot
And be incarnated in my thoughts
To where I truly belong

Amen!

ALL FOR SOMETHING

Reason is freedom
Freedom is natural
It is just a wish
A wish is the order
Order as driven by might
Never questioned or all rhetorical

Rights can never be inventions
Inventions are creations
Creations are discovered
Discovered in minds
Minds are inspired and inspiration is divine

LOVE LAMENTS

My heart was too stiff
I took a sniff
And coughed
All so rough
The side effects of sweetness

The complicacy
Laid it guilty
So I jumped and screamed
When her pupils beamed
We sold out to our souls

Where there is two,
Where it is a fight
Weary not of solitude
Weaving of all beautiful nothingness
In an ever hurting happiness

MOTHERLY

When I rode
Mum, on your back you allowed me
I sat on more than gold
Higher than the skies
Of the desert of "Futa Torroh"

That blanket
Wraps me warm in the cold
And so cold were all was hot
It has the mystics
Of the black woman
All in respect

Besides all what was the world
Where all you used to be
In the struggles of bare hands
Hard earned
Just to have us not surrender
In the eyes of hardship

In the darkness
Your eyes light up
For us to see at the end of the road
So we held hands
As brothers
We see the sisters
Who only know how to love us

So
In these feet I stand
In solid gratitude
For all that has been through us
In what's still a journey
Long indeed But with might

WHEN YOU LOOK INTO MY EYES

It should resemble the ocean
But through not color
As your eyes can't see
But your heart should know
Through my eyes
It should resemble yours
But not in content
It's where nothingness is a place
So you will rise

Through my eyes you should see
The diamond of the ocean but not blue
Not pyramid but shapeless
As it created the winds
Light and vision

Through my eyes
Only if you are blind
And dissolve in your quest
That you will see
That I resemble the ocean
But not blue!

WOULD YOU LIKE IT?

When the clothes don't wrap your body
To protect it from the winds and views
Would you like it?
I mean, when I choose not to see but your nudity

When you break the silence
When your voice calls for attention
That all have you in nails
And tight in screws
Would you like it?
I mean when I exaggerate your faulty wordings

What you do
Be what you demand
And earn perfection
So whether perfect
Or the other way,
Do not neglect the cat out of the bag
Before talking about people, ask yourself this:
"Would I like it to be said about me?"

MAY I NOT

I wish that there be none
That I ponder on none
But thee alone
Forever on

Let me not
Bring me thoughts
Of my deeds
As pride But blessing
Upon me

Let me
Forever lasting freedom
Not even think a seldom
About my being
But a dead ego
As life after death
Real life of the chosen ones

MAY I

In thy name
May I speak
May I do

In thy words
May I hear
May I ponder

In thy existence
May I feel
May I see

In my heart
May you be the fulfillment
That I realize

Yours in solitude
Living to die
So to live

GOLDEN RULE: THE POET

In his words:
In as much as you wish
Be, regardless of your ego
Keep all that speak from your heart
Not what you just mean in words
But in your doing
As you breathe,
Let what you live for
Be what you die for

Let all be praises
All for one
Glorify in solitude
The highest name, God
Where there is none
And yet where there is all
The all existing
And the all consisting

Rebel
Yes, repel all evil
That loudens the voice of deviants
And the path of the non-authentic
Break all the glasses
That they raise
And raise your faith
Solidarity on the right path

SOMETIMES

Sometimes
When I'm home alone
I cry, I shed tears, tears from my heart
So to ease up
The pain that got us
Whilst on the ride
That decides on the sides
Of what is success
And what it means to stumble

Sometimes
I lay on my bed
Whilst I rest in my room
That I so darkened
At least to give some loneliness
I so need to reminisce
In solitude, ascending
 In peace as I rest

Sometimes
When I'm not home alone
When I can't lay in my bed
When I can't darken my room
I just close my eyes
Spread my arms as wings
That I fly through time
Just to let me at ease
So as to carry on
To carry on ignoring this world
Which has turned to be an overload
Of distraction

ENSLAVED TEARS

It's only in the wind of no lands
I breathe, breathe in somber
Exhale all I have to hide
But hurt my deepest;
A thin thread I walk on
As in the valley of death
Since my regretted birth

My heart beats as I bleed
The tears that I dare not shed on my fore face
But drenched all deep within
The pain of amputation
That the umbilical cord witnessed
A wall that bind my feelings
Of being a son
At a tender age

In this field I grow
Only the cotton I harvest show me love
As they rub through and through my cracking palms
Whilst am on the treks pulling carts to fill
Under the watchful eye of the slave master
A self-proclaimed owner of me and my mother
A thief, as heartless as a rock

He crossed oceans and broke jungles
He found folks that sat on gold
That he crumbled and dispatched on a woeful voyage;
Journey of all deaths
But young men and women
In their virgin memories
They kept parcels
As my mother managed to keep me tales

She managed to pass on
What's my survival
As my foes look at me with a spiteful heart
That only shows me in the pictures
Pocks of regretted birth
Destined to live and die on the plantation
Without even an idea of self

It's been a long way before here
But too long we have to go from here
Well, until my demise that I am certain of
And then face my sins
That master had put me through;
Adultery like the horse
In stables when night falls
Blind intercourse that sees not
But an enslaved future for my sons and daughters
Like livestock, my kind was just needed in a huge number
To satisfy the manpower needed
Backed by greed and cruelty

HOW CAN I?

Gosh!
How can I ignore?
These smoky eyes
So dope, so high
Beyond the level of peaks
Rocky! Impossible for me to break

How can I not ignore
But for this charm
Eyebrows so soaked in beauty
That my eyelids rise
To the occasion of submission

How can I end this limbo?
Of a being that I live
That I cannot help
But keep striving
Serving and yearning
To swim and dissolve
In the ocean
That these eyes see from

AS YOU ARE

With all your darkness,
I see bright light
As I hear your crude voice
As the sweetest melody
And all your faults
For goodly, takes my judgment over
That you are of all

With all your dullness,
I see humbleness
Can't you for once appreciate my looks?
Even in the darkest hours,
I show your reflection
That you are up to perfection

Please don't let this die
For I wouldn't rest in peace
But do talk to me
I love you
Only for you
And as simple as you may be

GOING

Stove heated
Burning dope
Sour eyes
Can't pour tears
I mean no more
I don't want to

Misery still in that photo
Pulled off from the wall
Banged! Shattered!
This wall is so golden for pain
Stains of the past

So it shines
See us dine, smile and grind
The treasure we find
And show gratitude to him
The most kind
For choosing such a royal mama for my future

DESERTED ROSE

Again hear me cry
Deep from whispers
What I don't find right
But oppressed to so
To confess and take an oath
To reject what my desire yearns for

I know how it feels
In absence
So I appreciate the presence
That have so much moments
Lingering in motion
In my very best memoirs

Clouds melted
As promising as they did
They brought hard beats of thunder
And left me with a smiling sun
That only smiles not for me

I wish I had the knowledge of the eraser
As I was taught in kindergarten
Rub through and through
See off this painstaking…
Comics of a feeling
Hangs me in no seriousness

LONGING

It's empty
The hallow you left is square
And all the pegs to fill are round

How can I see more than I imagine?
Touch and respond to that smile
And make it mine

Come on!
Don't break this goblet
Take it as an offering
Fill it
Feel it
With all of yours
Indeed, it is yours
And you will never regret

GHETTO YOUTH'S CRY

I sail
Sail far in the Nile
I've covered miles
And spent time
But nothing I've seen makes me smile
Just a brother fighting another
Aids raping my sisters
The future darker
Children scream as they suffer
Yearning for food and water
Can't see a mother, nor a father
War had them all conquered
Now drought is taking over
Starvation and hunger

Deep in the eyes of a boy
Lying in the alley
Having to wake up early
From the remains of instability
Go drop some dope or pick pockets
Do whatever to get money
For survival is obligatory
And being the baby daddy,
He has to take care of my baby
And the baby mama is serving as a burden

I heard him pray: Oh lord
When will I live that perfect life?
Live in peace
Without the sound of guns and sirens

And no illicit means to survive
Build up the dream home
Be the father to my boy
To him, the daddy I never had
Let me not die hard
And rest in peace
To all those that have fallen hard

IF I COULD

If I could I would change the cards
That you'll lay hearts and minds
And let you utter my love

If I could I would break not this keyboard
But your silence
You speak sincerely
As much as I do, you will give me love

If I could,
My wireless would pull you
Drag you not
And "untwist" all that you feel
Make you the one on sight as I open my eyes

Feel you
Hold you and let me be yours
Get into your eyes
And your entire ocean, I will swim
Yes, if only I could

IF I COULD (II)

If I could be I would be yours
The one, the only one
That you will see and you touch
Get me by the lips
By the cool and cold
Let's rise from somber

If I could see
I'd prefer go blind
Never see us as two
But one of a whole
Complete retreat from the movies
Of the 'beauty and the beast'
Live the Jack and the Rose story
Even if we have to witness tragedy
Like the sinking of the Titanic
Defy the cons of the sinking ship
Let's play with the dolphins in the ocean
And the heart of the ocean

If I could talk
I would call your name
Speak deep in your heart
And tell her that my love spells your name
And ends my child play
And low, let hype be this love

But Oh!
This alone I wish for
But I can't
You alone I wish for
But tired of being in limbo
So, I rest in peace

SAKE FOR SAILING ON

After the skies are clear
The moon comes back to watch the stars
As they get illuminated
Sharpened and smiling
Readying to accompany the folk tales
At nightfall
Traces, of light
Left by the might
In the name of the sun
All of creation rise to her beauty

A mission not for a mason
Turned to be a game?
Either of the two am up for it
So, I play my cards on the table
All I got are hearts, diamond and spade
So, Lord feel me up with what they say
lord feel me up with what they say

Let the thrilling win dance
Dance and whistle to my tune
My dreams, my realities, my aspirations;
Peace, liberation, justice
For the skin I wear,
May it never wear out
But chocolaty more
As it smells, appear and speak
The eyes of the heroes and heroines
This is my will to see tomorrow!

HEARTY HALLOW

I wish I could write
A line of praise
To so dampen the memoires
Mold them, and build
Time ahead with your heart
I cut it short
I don't call on your calls
Not because of my sincerity to my true self
But my anxiety to stay true

I wish I could
Or just get null Than lose later
For a heart full Sold for gold
And a twilight's kiss

I mumble
The jungle without words
That even birds dear
And snakes dare
Daring to live deep below rocks
Oh so how I wish
To write a line of my thoughts
Say goodbye or welcome
All for good

IT'S A GOODBYE ROSE

This thing I'm throwing
I throw backwards
In as much we show our backs to one another
I wish that our backs never touched
For what lies on your vertebra
Is the flesh that made your tongue
Which pronounced all that's blown in the air
Never what you meant, is what you always said

Take this rose
A flower that hurts my deeper palms
With serious bleeding
Use it to ink your pen
Write my name beneath your feet
Step on me as you stabbed me in the back
Just forget that you saw me

Take this for good
For what has happened is not important
Let us lock horns no more
I have no strength to fight for this flimsy bite
Take this rose
That I grew with so much of my life
But have to let go
To erase all you embossed
Deep in my kindness
That only creates the channels
For the erosion of my manliness
On the note of your ending words,
It is a goodbye for good

LAMENTS; BLACK SKIN

When I was born,
In deep blackness
I saw nothing
I could only hear and feel
Only a being that I have been
True being, a soul so living

As growth came my way
Thoughts mama embossed
On what's a mindset
That even if she died or lived,
Purity remains in black

I remember that voice shouting
In silence echoing in the furthest
Hits the drums
Ears of sisters

Voices
Pronounce what I lament;
Deviation from the thoughts
Of my mama
They killed her
I see far with deep grief
A growing self-hate
Laments of a black skin

SOUL CHILD

I don't know how to talk
I've never seen
I can't even feel
I can't hear either
All I know is how to live
I left distance between
I and a stranger
Whose name I answered to
Whose life I led
Whose faith I preserved

He calls on my wishes
He grants me space
Of nothing but a breath
To stand and answer in the name of God

Souls channel through cracks in graves
In the midst of mountains
So ancient as worship
Never born
Never will I die
Because I am time
Flesh and blood doesn't define me

PABLO

Presence of a soul being
Absence of a hindering body
Broken casket
Lowered voices of the temporal
Origins of the mountains

I never did know you
Neither your body, nor your whereabouts
Rising, our souls knew where to meet
Under the droplets of a misty heart
Drenched the tears
Absolute silence in adherence

DEAR POET SALUTATION

Rising in respect
Of solitude
Of a being so incarnated
With what kind of thing
A life that you share a leaf
Away from speech in confidence

The circulation
Friction warmly wrapped
Raking all anonymousness
Sail through consciousness
Waking this sense of reasoning
Virtues of perseverance

Oh, this art!
That breathes me deep
I feel the unseen
Invokes of patience
Palms to cry on
Arms that feel my hugs

Dearly,
A being I never doubt
So strong in me
I fear not your end
For the poet never dies
With regards, I am the soul goblet
In quest for deepness and meaning

DESERT CLOUDS

So in bareness
Only in temptation
Crawling in impossibilities
Lost in the fields of no lands
Rotting seeds for a tomorrow

It's like all is desertion
Thought of the mountains
When all was smoke
That I all wished to climb on the peaks

Between the building blocks
Lies me as mud
Drying my whole being, holding blocks
Of a building which shelter not my very own son

The stone that the builder refused
A task like none ahead
For circumstances that guide all the way
Guard the odds all up for friction
Not between me and the valley of death

Man staggering in swagger
Out of pain so impure
Adaptive of this sinful life
A beak in the cycle
Chopping off a cracking skull
Running out of luck

Rest in peace
To that kid in dreams
All proved to be illusions
Like clouds in the desert
Which promise but never rain

SHALLOW ROOTED ROSE

Sigh of grips
Wrinkles of shadows
Gasping in wrapping
Passing, contemplating existence
Goddess of her kind
In her far gone statue
But gold of a hole

Loud voices as silent in a world
Of lost growing roses
So deeply rooted in fragility
Eden of complexity
Smiles of confusion

Excuse the goblet In the loss of rush
Barely finding this yearning
That is just yawning
Like that old cat
Hiding amidst the grass lands
Waiting for the rains
To bring some fish
But this is daydream
Skeletons of pain
Some emotional fractures

THE OPPOSITE OF AMEN

This solemnly lowering voice
Slowly breaking in silence
Bursting out of patience
Running out of luck

Perhaps these are the wishes
Mine and those of others
All for me
That I acknowledge in neediness
Turned me to a scape goat of prayer
So different from what I should have been

Maybe the raw facts of destiny
Had my points in the midst of success
Rather than this carved out valley of death
In which I laydown mortal

Now what's the opposite of amen?
A broom to sweep off the wishes
That make me temporal
Death in thought
But forever living in being
That is not prayed for
But wishes hinder

YOU DIDN'T GET WHAT I SAID

May be the skies have to open up
Rain only my clouds in thought
Then will you get it?
That still I doubt

I showed you my colors
You never saw me
For you let the atmosphere
Judge your vision
Where your personality hinders

Even if you don't get it
Or just want to glue strongly to your flimsy being
I still say what I said
In the loudest raw voice but sincere

To give you a reason
To keep it off your laments
I press the button
Keep the lights shining
On what's the self-esteem
Probably yours
That you don't understand me about

HOW TRUTHFUL ARE YOU?

You sing with the breeze
You write on the sky
You talk to the birds
You smile at the sun
But is it that you do it
Because you can never escape their sight?

So I wonder how timeless you are
As you said in your excuses
Or those are just a slight way
To get through me
Is it a joke?
Or just a wink for us to end it

Please convince me of your sincerity
Because even your jokes now hurt me
Or they are just a way to say "no thanks!"
You have better ways to run
That I don't even make in order
Order of your importance

How truthful are you?
Not a quarter as I love you
Please don't let me in the midst of doubts
For whatever being the truth,
I am happy to admit
Hard but I have the heart
For RIP is the best for the dead

NEAR FAILURE

Tasting the creamy present
That I saw from a distance
I was fooled by appearance
All that was so bitter
Now I know...

Glittered flawless
With a rusty inner
That is so much regret in one being
But whose fault is it, destiny?

Now, all the chances are in a thread
Running through that needle
Which bonds me with neediness
Which clinches me near failure

WHAT LIGHT HIDES

I know about something
That I really want to let out
But it can't be said
If said, can't be heard
If heard, it's just noise

I know about something
That I really want to get rid of
Try to show what it really is
But it can't be seen
If seen, it's a blank picture

I know about something
That can only be felt
That I feel myself
That explains it all in canvas
All fresh
Dressed within lines

This thing that I know
I can keep saying to you endlessly
And all I can, say is all that I know
I know about something
Because feelings can only be felt and never explained

SON, GOOD THINGS DON'T COME EASY

A day that so left me a hallow
I woke up before the sun
And I died in chants
Read me
What the mighty speaks

Fresh in as it shines
I see it in your eyes
Your eyeballs are the sun
The luminosity in the house
That we all see with ease

Son,
I felt you
Having to sacrifice this young age
Being indifferent with all other sons of the moment
Painting a picture that answers to your name

It so takes a lot
Both you and I
The whole of us
As we live through time
I shall whisper in your ears
What my heart speaks
This unbreakable bond
Of being in love with everything

Son,
The distance in between
Knows not the further we see
For our hearts know exactly where to meet
No matter if it's night or day
Just live in might
And hear me say
Good things don't come easy

RISE WITH THE TRUTH

Rise up
In this morning
Of hidden agenda
Smiles as fake as the realities
This world of classes
That begets the three walls
Division of a world
To man's sudden misery
Stands facing each other
Of brothers and sisters

Rise up
Realize what is fishy in the story
Challenge the laws; loopholes
Listen to yourself
You can identify what's gold
For lies can be invisible
But can be identified
You just need to be sincere

Rise up
From the trap
The system is a stem
Which ignites self-hate in you
A tomorrow in limbo

Rise up
Free your mind from the media
Don't let the news make you hyper
Our yesterday is not dead
So we live in incarnation
Never can death stop us
Rise up son
Raise up the sun
For waiting are our sons
Let tomorrow not wait

EMPT

Again, a bag full of air
That can't dry my wet hair
In this moment of despair
Or let me say, stabs
Sandy on the back
Straight into the spine
My thoughts are crumbled

An empty space
A barrier before the grass
 Cattle have to graze
But the grace of a man fell off
In the gutters of dalliance
In the midst of limbo

In cold, so bare
Like the open earth
In the desert of aspirations
A wealthy head of dreams
Here, I stand on no feet
Not ready but needy
To start from zero

LIVE UP BLACK BROTHER

What else could I wear but gold
If it's all I knew and held
Felt the ever living
On the might of the peaks
On the throne of Najasi
And in the mind of Shankara
Peace and respect I never lack
Simplicity and respect I have in packs

Dear Black child
Wipe your tears
And realize that you are no different
But all that I am, you are
No more are you going to die
No more are you going to live in refugee camps
Listen to me
And you shall hear what's within
That thing that fills the emptiness
They carved it out from your history

Black youth,
Drink from the Nile and keep calm
The mental prison is broken
The slave ship has drowned
And the black star line is on shore
We'll get back home soon
And surely find light
If not sunlight, but twilight
We'll go star gazing and paint our sky
I mean our very own
From red, gold and green
The colors would never defy

Black youth
My brother in the ghetto
You 'll soon not be jailed for being you
Though they label you hoodlum
I know you seek to make ends meet
Nothing else stirs up the desire to do
They should crap those laws that are stranger
Break those barriers
Get to school and learn the roots
Kill the cause for frustration
Trade our gold
As our goal in the days of Mansa Musa
Live up black brother
Live up!

BLACK NATION

In this so black,
I see lines so clear
Lines that track the right path
It is the land of my birth
The land of humanity's birth
The land of faith, belief, strength
The land of life
Riches of the world; smiles

Black nation
Where it takes a village to raise a child
Where every man is a father
And every woman a mother
For a youth to grow stronger
In the highest peaks of Kilimanjaro
Waterfalls of respect
This dwells in even the birds
Chanting in the Congo woods
And echo as far as the Sahara

It takes not one to unite,
But many to form a union
Diversity makes us many
As we live in peace and unity
It is our strength to live on
So we pray and hold on
Black for life
We mean life
The royalty is our reality
That we will pass to the next century

What a strong people
Who survived all these struggles
Bombs and guns that we never know how to make
Brought to us war and dismay
From slavery to the struggle for freedom
Democracy has never made it better
But we shall rise

Sons and daughters of our nation
Rise up from confliction
We are no slaves
But kings and queens of kin
In this holy land
Full of spiritual vibes and strength
That leaves not it's sons
That the sun never leaves
It's the black nation
Our nation
So we rise!

MY STAND

Two decades ago
When my brother was still in Guantanamo
I grew up surviving my challenge of life
Depicting me, since I was not alive
A picture that was all facades

For so long are years
When in the waves, my ears were caught
That I heard the mainstream media
They brought me fear and self-hate
That when I hear about Ethiopia,
I think of hunger
And all the pictures I see of Sudan
Are of war and anger
I was never showed the bright side of Egypt
But Tahrir square when tribulations gripped

Hadn't I had a clue of media bias
I would have believed that our heroes aren't heroes
And our foes are our heroes
They want me to hate the ones who love me
And love the ones who wronged me
That's the media's strategy to control me

All these, we the suns of time have to realize
Our religions are guides and not barriers
And our ethnicity gives us the strength to unite
Listen to everything

But mindful of what goes into your mind
For our destruction is someone's passion
And he is what he appears not to be
You just have to stand for something
I mean that thing which you are
Everything that is you
Stand and raise your head
So you wouldn't fall for anything

BLUE DAY FLOWER

Even the skies were so friendly
That all the clouds melted
And gave the sun a peep of the earth
The earth, so gloomy
The day in a blue moon
Even the mountains trembled
Gave patches and channeled some water
Waterfalls and rivers
Connected the 'oceanic' earth

Reels on the hottest mountains
That were snow now sunny
On this blue day,
The whole world is in summer

This day
Grew all at once
I harvested from the hands of the Lord
I let go and hold on
For this I've got
Not every day is blue,
So I rejoice
And cherish my adorable rose

LINGERING FAILURE

Ask me about life
Ask me about love
Ask me about my people

I will tell you about hardship,
I shall tell you about deception,
I shall tell you about division

Never proving man's brotherhood
A prove of monkey's royalty
Dancing to the tune of greed
Whilst the populace pays the price of the music

Don't ask where we are heading to
For never can one fall up
We've been pulled by this gravity
Was it our invention?

Sons of time, let's stop asking
And answer the questions
That have been lingering
Let's pass it not
To the children of our nation

DESPAIR

Hope slipped
Fell and broke
When I slept
My soul soaked
In the depths of confusion
Still motion
Blank stare
At this irony of being

Love,
Spilled under my feet
Fell and broke on the grill
Still burning under the skins of ambition
Exposed to hazards of reality
Failure is near
Not a dream, a fear

At dusk
When birds fly back to nests
Clouds see the sun
Below the horizons of the west
I still gasp in the mist of struggle
Blossoms of broken
Eggs counted before hatching
Turned out to be rotten

I'M DEAD, DON'T REMEMBER ME

I'm dead
Don't say RIP
Don't remember me
Don't bury me

Just let me be
I'm not your corpse
You 're not my undertaker
You cannot let me in to heaven
For when you saw me pegged
Down the lane of failure
You saw the hand I waved
But never handed me a hand of help
Don't bury me
Don't even call me names
For they are worldly
I'm a son of heaven
And the graves are hell

Don't remember me
Don't engrave my names on a tomb
Don't remember my birthday
Don't think of where I'm going to stay
Don't cry over my demise
For I never meant a thing
Just pulses that never meant
A thing to our world

Lord, hear me speak
From the depths of a heart
In this quest
That impossibility still burning
Eating up my chest
My stand; my whole being

HARD TIMES

The times when you question fate
When you start asking
Pronouncing those words
From the depths of pain
"Why me?" you ask in plea
On the face of all the tribulations
It is time never moving
Or moving fast with friction
Against your throat
Threatening to deviate
From the truth of being

These times
When you can't rise up against the odds
When you think of yourself odd
When you are tired of prayer
When you are silent
When you think God is silent
When you think God hears no more
Or don't have eyes for you
I mean ears for your wishes
These times
When all you have is "take heart"
When even hope is slipping off
When success is written off
From your destiny,
It's all mystery
When no one cares
Because they don't even know
Like that burning field
Way far in the abandoned lands

Brother,
Again, you will hear take heart but from me
That's different because it's from a heart
He who feels it,
They say knows it
I feel our being, we are dying
This is our story that I am representing
Sincerely, from the ghetto

SPLITTING WINTER

Living
Hard turns the shapeless
Sour turns the tasteless
Emerging with the freshness
Even the corpse of fishes
And that of every living being

Like the sun decides on time
Revolves the earths to be hear
Winds so powerful; tornado
Like that hissing snake
Swallowing the eggs of events
The sacred and the secrets

Dying
Falling leaves
Leaves the flora
Stands in skeletons
Upright showing might
Fasting for emancipation
Only the dying lives
Forever on in this split

Meeting
After comes the regime
Which dwells through time
With freshness all over earth
Blossoms
Dressed in plain cotton;
It is all solidified liquid
That is the meaning

LIVING WISH

He isn't god
We are God's
For we're nothing but what exists
In plain, not in vain
Felt, not seen
Seen when felt
When the veils tear
And light prevails

Find us outside when the sunrises
Rest in peace at twilight
Ascending souls higher than the zenith
Plugged to the electric charges of life
Living in connection with the depths and the height
Living the life of not just this world

May he grant us virtue
Guidance to the perseverance of the sacred!

SOW THE SEED IN MY WORD

Bury your seed
In the earths at last
For a true and lasting merry
Through you, be the happiest

Bury your seed
I swear I will shower the rains
For its upkeep and growth
Survive the strong storms
Hold the earth from crumbling

Pour it out
In a jar of earth
This earth in the midst of my palms
So enriched and yearning
For that seed from divine
Grow to witness until the sun shines

As you hear,
I wish you tear
All the doubts and fears
Let this grow straight
In a blink like a spear

The shiniest it appears
In as much you whisper
Let it be trust
Because this is true

LETTER

Since nobody understands,
Somebody wants to understand
Did he ever listen to me?
Could she understand the realm?
Oh, no
It's not something physical
It's a feeling over me

So I write with plight
A terrible situation to feel the hallow within my inner
And no eyes to see the colors of the rainbow
See me write
Feel my thoughts
As I confide in you, my Lord
You know what I mean
This unexplainable feeling of you,
Only we can understand

I salute
Pardon me, for that I should have done first
But yet still, I was meant to be
That I understand
As I bow...
The purest manifestation of my feelings
And adherence to the decree

In a note
You said I was the destined
The piece of earth in life
Through time, breaking out from the shells
My conclusion is unknown
Even by me, a son of time
And time is still on

Still unknown
Whatever becomes the conclusion,
I bowed and here I bow
What comes next, you have time
Until then, through the while,
Yours lover,
Servant of the merciful

I AM ANCIENT

Leaving modernity
Living the ancient mystics
Aged son of time
Reflections of divine light
Within the east western:
Son of the easterner that rose from the west

Still living the moments
Of when the world was still young
Before the stars ascended
It's an echo
Of what's not heard by many
It has taken over my ears,
And conquered my being

My philosophy is ancient
Much like when the earth was flooded
I witnessed Noah explore the tides
The start of our day
A long day of real men:
I name the friend that chanted the names
Which were beautiful

It's golden: it shines
Not because of color
But for a hard, smooth and shiny surface
Rocky in the rocks
Forever living
For I am ancient

HEAR OUT

Now would you listen,
Can you hear?
There are voices from under the bridge;
Cries from the world of the disadvantaged
A world in the world
Never having a voice
Because they never mean economic benefit

The capitalist's state of mind is less human
A thick forest will have to be deforested
Just for the sake of money
And education turned to a wealthy business
Making it expensive for these people
There seems to be no way out with this

I hope that the system will be selfless someday
And realize that in the event of a deserted world,
With no life,
Depopulated and deserted
All the wealth will be meaningless
For gold, silver, petroleum and money cannot be eaten
And then, it will be the end of all the hustle with meaninglessness

SOMETIME IN HELL

With a heavy heart
Tears rolling up to my knees
I am down and going down
Reminiscing in pain
Resting the blame
I so regret the fame

Bald headed
My hair burnt
In no time,
I was to be ashes
All alone to bear the lashes
Back and front
Computing my pulses
Counting on my last breath
To set me free

A hard reality
Story of an unborn child
Destined to go wrong
Some cloth in flames
Naked in the cold
A sin to think bold
Lingering in folds
Without caption;
Pictures of bygone

CRIES

Out loud in pain becomes a joy
To see water in this desert
Are tears for a relief
From fear and pain
Of the days when man was the villain

Dry cries
Shouts of the heart
Without voices
Read in the eyes
Of the vulnerable
Convicts of destiny
Enslaved by birth
Misery unfazed
When light sheds
On the huddles further

Riding on mothers' backs
To shelter from the storm
Raining cats and dogs
From the hinter lands
That would bite and chew on me
In this atmosphere of cold fight
Tomorrow's might in limbo

Hearts going out
To victims of civilization
On the edges of the mines
In limbo, waiting for the inevitable
The doom of generations
Crying out blood
For life, a matter living
Hoping to reach the bigger ears

VIBES AT DUSK

Feeling the sharp breeze
Hear the ocean tides
It's the sun I see again
Witnessing the setting
Atmosphere of optimism

It is another day
Man buckling up
As the bells ring
Alarm for time
With stars ever bright
A moment of twilight;
A deep expression for love
Forgetting and in regret
For what man makes of himself

Wishes shining
Like sparkling stars
In their numbers
High up in the sky
So every man looks high
Showing each other the brightest clusters

On the peaks,
I am so looking at these stars
Sincere about what I show;
Stay longer, holding hands
Jibe with life before sunset
Just before time
It's a last glance of the sun
Completion of a revolution
A life time witness
So I rejoice in my presence

Wishes in the long run
Giving up the long fight
A moment of silence
Respect to time
A law of Mother Nature
Destiny's part in the game

Feeling the last breeze
Westward winds
Witnessed in the far east
Down here waiting for time
It's the last breath
The end marks the start

Ruled in the far past
Forgiving is an obligation
A medium of might
Simplicity taking pride
It's all in
No raising of glasses
But a raise of the head
In time, we are freed

NOTHING FELT

Looked at the mirror
Saw me horrific
Man in half
The little boy
And the old bitter man

Looked at the mirror
Saw nothing similar to me
A rotten brain man really had
That all along smelled
Like fragrance lied the nose

All along I adhered to lies
I am nothing
That I never knew
Even my eyes fooled me

I want to go blind
Become a deaf person
Because I trust not my eyes and ears
Let me feel being nothing
For I am nothing

TWILIGHT

Got me see the skies
That has no endings
Full of sparkling stars
Shedding on my marshy lands
A plan that I would always adapt
To rain on me
My ego is eroded
I am logged me with love
My thoughts proved
My dead heart resurrected
And buried my illusions
Then on,
Peace ever flourished
Me, a bitter sweet man
Having reasons to cry
Reasons to cheer
Appreciating me
For being me
A justification for my action

BITTER PRESENCE

Lost my voice
To the vultures of no land
Evolved man landing on thin clouds
Defecating on my head provoking my clemency
With soldier arms, bony legs, pegged in darkness
Man is a fat brain fed with pride
Doomed their days nothing they pay
Loaded with anger crawling on lands, bare
A desert elephant
Looked low upon like and ant
Casting shadows on the forecast
A doomed day

WRONG STEPS

Blaming God
For making you yourself
Regrets in vain
Thoughts of the insane
Taught by ultimate stupidity
Utmost complexity
Souls in brutality
Homemade inferiority
Continuous combustion
Fueled by our very own youth
To the last drop of blood
Sacrifices of the soul
In the eyes of synthetic gods
Without a reward;
A slave of the slave
The most desperate of slaves
This is no hyper
A bitter of generations
A wrong interpretation
Of our ancestors' dreams
Sour turns the cream
Failed is the dream;
The independence decade

BEFORE I DIE

Should I say my last wish?
Yes! Let peace flourish
Pain vanish
And Satan be banished
This would be my wish after my demise,
My people jibe to the highest vibe
Save the soul from the last riddle

If I were to wish at last,
Heaven would be my last
But repent on the past
Get you back fast
And we live on to last

My wish shouted out
Louden the voice of my people's choice
Answering not in my name but ours
Let light shine one the land
Sunrise for the people